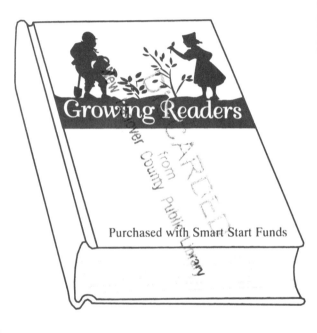

Character Education

Self-Discipline

by Lucia Raatma

Consultant:
Madonna Murphy, Ph.D.
Associate Professor of Education
University of St. Francis, Joliet, Illinois
Author, *Character Education in America's*
Blue Ribbon Schools

Bridgestone Books
an imprint of Capstone Press
Mankato, Minnesota

Bridgestone Books are published by Capstone Press
151 Good Counsel Drive, P.O. Box 669, Mankato, Minnesota 56002
http://www.capstone-press.com

Library of Congress Cataloging-in-Publication Data
Raatma, Lucia.
    Self-discipline/by Lucia Raatma.
    p. cm—(Character education)
    Includes bibliographical references and index.
    Summary: Explains the virtue of self-discipline, or controlling your actions, and
describes ways to show your self-discipline at home, at school, and in the community.
    ISBN 0-7368-0511-7
    1. Discipline—Juvenile literature. 2. Self-control—Juvenile literature.
[1. Discipline. 2. Self-control.] I. Title. II. Series.
BJ1533.D49 R33 2000
179'.9—dc21   99-048336

Editorial Credits

Sarah Schuette, editor; Steve Christensen, cover designer and illustrator;
    Kimberly Danger, photo researcher

Photo Credits

FPG International LLC/Jeff Baker, cover; Jeffrey Sylvester, 18
International Stock/Elliot Varner Smith, 4; Jeff Greenberg, 20
Matt Swinden, 8, 10, 12, 14
Frances M. Roberts/Richard B. Levine, 6
Unicorn Stock Photos/Aneal Vohra, 16

1 2 3 4 5 6   05 04 03 02 01 00

Table of Contents

Self-Discipline 5

Being Self-Disciplined. 7

Self-Discipline at Home 9

Self-Discipline with Your Friends 11

Self-Discipline in Sports 13

Self-Discipline at School 15

Self-Discipline in Your Community. 17

Florence Griffith Joyner 19

Self-Discipline and You. 21

Hands On: Make a Daily Schedule 22

Words to Know 23

Read More 24

Internet Sites 24

Index. 24

Self-Discipline

Self-discipline means doing what you should. You show self-discipline when you work to meet your goals. You show self-discipline by doing your chores before playing. Being self-disciplined will help you become successful and independent.

goal
something that you plan for
or work toward finishing

Being Self-Disciplined

Self-disciplined people take good care of themselves. You can show self-discipline by doing things to stay healthy. You can exercise and eat foods that are good for you.

Self-Discipline at Home

You show self-discipline at home by following the rules. Self-disciplined people put their responsibilities before having fun. Finish your chores without being reminded. You can earn your family's trust when you do what you should.

responsibility
a duty or job

Self-Discipline with Your Friends

Spending time with friends can be fun. But sometimes you may disagree with your friends. Self-disciplined people control their behavior. Try to use calm words when you are upset. Walk away to calm down instead of fighting.

behavior
the way someone acts

Self-Discipline in Sports

Doing well in sports is hard work. Maybe you want to be a soccer player. But you are not a good kicker. You show self-discipline when you practice your skills. You show self-discipline when you keep trying.

Self-Discipline at School

Being self-disciplined at school will help you learn. You are self-disciplined when you listen to your teacher instead of talking. You are self-disciplined when you study for a test. You show self-discipline when you finish your homework before watching TV.

Self-Discipline in Your Community

A community is a good place to live when people control their behavior. Self-disciplined people obey laws. They clean up the community instead of drawing graffiti. Self-disciplined people make your community a nice place to live.

graffiti
pictures or words painted or written on someone's property without permission

"I have lost more races than I have ever won. I learned from defeat and used it to improve."
—Florence Griffith Joyner

Florence Griffith Joyner

Florence Griffith Joyner was an athlete from the United States. She trained and practiced running. Her self-discipline helped her become a successful runner. She won five medals in the Olympic Games in 1984 and 1988. She set world records in two events.

Olympic Games

sports contests among athletes from many countries

Self-Discipline and You

You are responsible for your behavior.
Learn to balance your responsibilities
with having fun. Being self-disciplined
may help you meet your goals. You
will be successful and independent if
you use self-discipline.

Hands On: Make a Daily Schedule

Self-disciplined people plan their activities so they can finish them on time. You can make a schedule to help you plan your day.

What You Need

Two pieces of paper
A pen or pencil

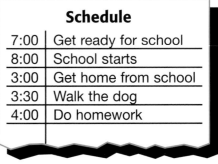

What You Do

1. On the first piece of paper, make a list of the tasks that you must get done each day. Include tasks such as going to school, doing homework, and doing chores.
2. Draw a line down the other piece of paper. Write times of the day on the left side of the line.
3. Write the tasks you need to complete on the right side of the line. Start with tasks that are always at the same time, such as going to school.
4. Choose other times to do your homework or chores. Write these tasks next to the times you plan to do them.
5. Complete your tasks at the times you scheduled. You can check them off when you finish. You will get everything done if you follow your schedule.

Words to Know

behavior (bi-HAYV-yuhr)—the way a person acts

goal (GOHL)—something that you plan for or work toward finishing

graffiti (gruh-FEE-tee)—pictures or words painted or written on someone's property without permission

independent (in-di-PEN-duhnt)—free from the control of other people or things

responsibility (ri-spon-suh-BIL-uh-tee)—a duty or job

schedule (SKEJ-ul)—a plan for completing a task or job

Read More

Gambill, Henrietta. *The Child's World of Self-Control.*
Plymouth, Minn.: Child's World, 1997.
Rutledge, Rachel. *Women of Sports: The Best of the Best in Track
& Field.* Brookfield, Conn.: Millbrook Press, 1999.

Internet Sites

Adventures from the Book of Virtues—Self-Discipline
http://www.pbs.org/adventures/Storytime/selfDisc.htm
Florence Griffith Joyner
http://www.cmgww.com/sports/joyner/joyner.html
Self-Discipline
http://www.motivationmaster.com/newpage2.htm

Index

athlete, 19
chores, 5, 9
goals, 5, 21
graffiti, 17
homework, 15

Joyner, Florence
   Griffith, 19
laws, 17
Olympic Games, 19
practice, 13

rules, 9
soccer, 13
study, 15
test, 15
trust, 9